Pretty skin

Sana mian

Pretty skin
Copyright © 2018 Sana Mian

ISBN-13: 978-0692178072
ISBN-10: 0692178074

Contact Information:

Instagram: __sanamian__
Email: miann.sana@gmail.com

Thank you, Hasan, for being the friend that I've always needed. Thank you for listening to me whenever I've needed to speak, and thank you for never telling me to stop.

I love you from the wholeness of my heart

For the girls
Finding homes
In books
And themselves

What you'll find:

:

Without God
I am
But, thin layered skin
Running around
On this loudish blue
Earth

It has never
Slowed down
It's time for me

Age: 24

I've started loving the sun
The summer and it's winking lights
Keep me happy
It's unusual
Because I have never been
Fond of the summer
It's when people love coming out
They love showing themselves

- and that has been the hardest task of my life

Could I tell you about
Myself
I'm a flower child
I wear those little finger plants in my hair
And admire them in their roots
Without grabbing
At times
I'm trying
I'm trying
I'm a soldier child
Ready to survive
The news you deliver to me
I'm a feisty woman
I've learned from the women
Around me
I have pretty skin
I wear sun dresses
In yellow flickering light
All dressed up,
Nowhere to go,
A flower child
Who has pretty skin
I'm obsessed with being you
And I'm obsessed with being me

- first day, introductions

The weight machine says
Something, different
Compulsive liar
Every time
I step on it
Like bipolar women
Who can't quite
Stick with decisions
Sometimes
The pointer leans
To the right
And some days
It runs to the left
It's a tug of war on my scale
It depends on
The month, the year
And my stress levels

- i binge eat at midnight

Starvation at fifteen

I find hair coming off
My scalp
As I come of the age
Like too many people
Getting off the train
At once
No patience
You'll find them clogging
Up the drains
So, we have the plumber over
At least once a week
There as thick as the
Loose strands of
My house mop
That are found lying
On the marble floors
Of my wet room
After a vigorous
Day of spring cleaning

They surrender to the comb
That my mother
Aims into the stubborn knots
Of my tangled cobweb hair
Thin as the alzheimer patient
That I took care of
In downtown brooklyn
During high school
And as weak as the reach
Of his memory
And I'm as as confused and helpless
As him,
When he was first brought there
By his most favorite child

- is this part of puberty

He asks me
What sort of man
Am I to you
And I allow
The words to
Flow out
As sweet
Syrup

You're a man who doesn't ask
If it's a yes or a no
A man who tells you all the
Questions that you're allowed to ask
A man who doesn't let you choose
Because he was born to choose better
A man who doesn't know how
To be a man

But, he didn't lick his fingers after

I'm dancing
Slowly
I'm rubbing myself against
The wind
Because, it doesn't hinder
It allows you to be free
To move however
I'm doing it deliberately
In my short yellow dress
That gives the promise
Of wide rich hips
That are perfect for you to touch

And now
Too many things
Happen at once
I'm working at seven eleven
And the line keeps getting longer
And I don't even know how to use
The register
Because it's my second day here
So, more people keep appearing
Like distant acquaintances,
When they hear of your success,
And everyone's angry now,
And I'm calling for my supervisor and
He's nowhere to be seen
I can't keep up with everything
Even though, I'm a woman
Multi tasking queen
So, instead,
I sway my shoulders
Then I twirl
And twirl

Age 23

Maybe, I'm not grateful enough
I'm oblivious
I should make a list of all the good
I have a running faucet
I know that they have bigger problems
But, I don't know how
To handle mine anymore

Age: 14

Closing the door shut
I worry if it's like the others
Stretched out across my bed
With my knees wide-open
I lay like how my mother laid
When she gave birth to me
And my siblings
And like how my legs open
When I find myself in my room
On a lonely friday night
I lean in

There's a mirror hovering just
Above my thigh
And I angle it to find the opening
Is this what it's supposed to look like
I stick my hand onto the surface
To trace the velvety ridges and mound
Its smooth, but rough in other places
Like there's little beads inside my skin
I find the opening and slide my finger in
To see if it's the correct size
I don't know what the correct size is
But, my hole seems too small
I panic
I'm confused
I retreat
But, I do it again
I reach far into the darkness
Looking for my period
This new foreign part of my body
Is it like the others

- late bloomers

First shave

My face is a field
Made for growing hair
My face is a sun bear
Furry
Even prickly
My sideburns resemble the jewish boys
That I've grown up around
The ones with small black hats glued
To their heads
Hat's that have vowed to never slip off
Even when they run against the wind
My aunt wants my sister
And I to come over
So, my mother decides that
I should trim the green grass near my lips
Similar to vacuuming lint
Covered carpets
She gets rid of the hair
Now, it's red
And it hurts
I think everyone would know
I had hair there before
My face is a field of grass
With balding
Above my lips
I look horrible
But, I'm too full of myself to notice

- that ovary syndrome

15

My body has dots
Everywhere
You could lay with me
The entire day
Connecting them
Like the stars that you connect
To see kites in the sky
So many patterns
On my milk tea skin
They call them sweet fruit
Strawberries
So, is it the reason
You suck on my skin
To taste the sweetness

- are they sweet enough

Teenager

My hair isn't as full anymore
So, I get shorter haircuts
To make them seem fuller
Like, when you spread out
Food on your plate
To feel like you're eating
Alot
Or, when you count your blessings
And thank God for running water
Covering your belly with a
Pillow, when you eat
So you don't notice
The effect your mindless eating
Has had on your body,
Now, I notice the hair loss
Shampoo commercials on t.v.
They make sense now
They say garnier fructis
Works wonders
But, it doesn't work for me
I'm a girl
Experiencing a bad hair day
Except, it's months, now
Autumn doesn't end
I noticed, woman are intense about
The width of their ponytails
They say you're as beautiful
As the the thickness of your hair

- being enlightened

17

Age 16

I wear jeans
That aren't my size
Like my shoes
Are a size smaller
So, they claw into
My hips and leave
Red bumpy roads
Around my waist
I don't like fitting into
My own size
So, I don't raise my hand
In class, when I know
What the professor
Is going to answer later
That's being big
And women aren't
Supposed to be big
They're supposed
To be small
And dainty
So, they could be held
So, I shrink myself
And mask my mass
Behind the boy
Sitting in front of me

- imposter syndrome

18 makes you legal

He asks me if I hate him
Because he agitated
My mind, and my body
He adores my never ending thoughts
But, I don't know what to say
I don't know what to hate of someone
Who seems troubled, too
He tells me, he hates me
With an electric anger
It travels through wires
Unnoticed
His voice is lower in sound
When it was supposed to be high
He was supposed to be shouting
Like my dad when he's angry
On the phone
With my mother's brothers
He's caressing my neck with lotion
He wants to fix things
By rubbing me
The right way
In this passenger seat
He bit my neck
And he says it was love
It's now a mark of love
Something pure, full of love
Like a lover's lock
Hanging off a bridge
It's a symbol now
Like question marks
When you're curious
I'm not happy
I don't feel happy
But, I'm not sad

I'm sitting across this woman
In this claustrophobic
Metallic colored office
I've been here before
Because of a car accident
When I was younger
But, then I came with
My dad
She's supposed to be asking me
Important questions
About what I did with him that day
I feel guilty already
Because I did like him
But, I wouldn't tell that to my dad
Because then he wouldn't believe me
So, she asks me how I was pinned down
Was it just his hands pinning me down
Or was it the whole body weight
And I think she wants
To figure out if I'm lying
Like women who falsely accuse
And send black men to jail
For decades
Ending their football careers
But, I'm not that
But, I feel like it
And I would tell her
But I'm so afraid
Like little boys who start stuttering
Because of angry fathers
Because I did like him
I try finding an answer to one of her questions
But, what is the correct answer
She says it seems like I'm battling in my head

- i have been

I am growing, boy
In the
Beginning
Stages
Of blooming, boy
Like a flower
Twirling up
To the sun
That is still so far
A stretch in the morning in bed
Slowly
Hands reaching out
Waking up
Taking it's time
Twirling up
To illumination
Of thought
And awareness of self
Till it's full height
And space
I'm learning
I'm making sense
I don't want your hungry eyes
I don't want your hard kisses
I don't want your pushes
I don't want to be cornered
Here and there
I am growing
In the beginning
Stages
Of blooming
Please
Let me finish first

Why do they make you feel
Shame and guilt
For something that you didn't do
For something that was done to you
For something handed and not chosen
If I had the choice, I wouldn't choose it

- questions

High school

I travel on six trains a day
In New york city
Because I can't stay in school
There are too many questions there
I never want to answer them
The man that I love doesn't talk to me
The woman that I love doesn't talk to me
I walk around the five boroughs
Aimlessly
I don't talk to me

- 24 hour quiet zone

The dress that I wore twice
The one that is strange
A combination of orange and pink
Peachy
With dots
Is still hanging in my closet
It's pushing its way to the front
Of the line
When my closet creaks open
With paranormal activity
I see it peaking
To get my attention
My dress is just like me
I still remember how soft
It felt against my skin
I wore it with you
You said I looked very traditional
That's how you liked your girls

Age 7

Still eyes looking at you
They're magnificent
My mother bought me one for my birthday
We went straight to the store when I came
Back from school
This one looks like a real baby
It also has a opening where its mouth is
So, we could feed it milk
It looks so real
Babies are so cute
I want a baby
Mother says that God leaves them
For us on window sills
In the morning time
I think I'll get one too, soon
If I let him do what he does
I don't mind him
But, I'd rather go eat
But, I want a baby
I'd bring it to school with me
In my bookbag
And it would be just mine

I can't focus anymore
I can't put my mind
Around a habit
And sit with it

I forget about it
I put my hand
Around it
Instead
And I choke
It

- early endings

18 makes you legal

They always ask me
Why I came back to you
Even after
I gravitated to you like a moth to white light
You were the light
Because you read me
You thought about me
You said you loved me
And that is all that I've ever really wanted

- attention seeker

Age 23

I came to his house
To meet him after years
He has the sort of face
That you could trust
Baby face, childlike innocence
A man from a good family

We drink his favorite rum
And when I wake
I am brown flesh
Under his comforter

Someone shouted fire
In the movie theater
Everyone's screaming
So, lets run

I want to hold his comforter
Against me
As much as I want to throw it away
And I want to hold my flesh against me
As much as I want to throw it away

He tells me that I wanted it
As much as he did
And I don't remember
I don't want to make a scene
Because he behaves like everything's fine
So, I believe him
And behave like everything's fine

- it doesn't feel fine, I feel hungry

I don't believe anything
I tell myself
I ask people about
Myself instead

- self hatred

18 makes you legal

You were supposed to be
The woman of my dreams
The one who would sit with me on porches
On windy, summer days
We'd hold each others fingers
Like paper clips connected
For longer than lovers get to hold hands
And walk to the train station
Instead of taking the bus
After school
Listening to music
A headphone for me
And one for you
Because the weather was always nice
And it took the same time
But, you just left
I told you to go
When I needed you
And you left
I thought you felt
What I felt
And never showed
My words were thorn
Because of frustration
And what the world
Handed to me
I thought you'd know that
My heart was always rose petals for you

- you will always be my greatest heartbreak

18 makes you legal

The day that I told my mother
Of what you did to me
She called my dad
He was at work
She didn't tell him right away
She told him to come home first
She was so calm
Her chest seemed stiff
As if she was wearing a warrior's armor
And that made me wonder
Of how many times she had
Delivered bad news
To be so good at it

- mother

Dads should've given birth
If mothers were given all the emotions
To balance the scale

- two parents

When Dad gets angry
He raises his voice so loud
Until all the children run home
From the playground
Until all the flowers begin to shrink
Back into the ground
Don't want to be seen
And the air hides away
From my lungs
Still
Mute women

He goes to visit
Her
Every Friday
She hasn't been his mother
For the last forty years

- favoritism in grandmothers

Binghamton University

You're right
I have two things to do
School and work
They should fill
The space that
I take up
But, I haven't been
Able to do either
I've been running round
And around
In the same direction
Like the ride in my school
In Pakistan
That would get you dizzy
To the point of not being able
To stand right after
And the
Tree game that i would
Play with my best friend
In first grade
Run around and around
Until someone gets caught
I think more than I do
And I show
Less than I care
And the clock
Keeps ticking
And the damn suns out again

I have the hardest time
Having women as friends
I cover my face with my short haircut
Whenever they come by
To look aloof
And eye them
From my peripheral vision
And wear red lipstick
To look distant
And close the door shut
On their faces
Whenever they speak
Because I don't think I deserve your love

- because she made me believe that

The year I got sexually assaulted
Was a year I thought would end time
I couldn't see a future, because well
Life didn't go as I planned for it to
And it was supposed to be a certain way
And then it wasn't that certain way
So, the world had stopped working correctly
It was damaged now
Like when you accidentally drop your phone in water
After that, you kinda just wait for it to die out
But, months passed by
And then we were
A few months into the next year
And I was still living,
And the world was still working fine
People were graduating high school
Moving away to college
Speaking about their dreams and the goals
That they were going to accomplish
It was unusual that the world was happy
When I hadn't been
I was still the person
Who had gotten sexually assaulted
But, the world was still working fine
I felt hopeful now too
In hindsight, it felt as if
As i was living through the year
Someone in the background was fixing the world
Maybe, fixing the lens that I viewed the world with
Maybe, giving the glass a good rub
Maybe, it was distance
Maybe it was time
Maybe it was God
But, it started feeling like I belonged again

Dear you
I think the first boy who says
That he cares about you
Holds a responsibility towards you
He has to be on his best behavior
Always
The way that he treats you is how you
Identify the face of intimacy
You showed me
That if I wanted to be loved and kept
And taken care of
I'd have to kiss rubbery lips on days
That I wasn't sure if I wanted to
And lay with people
Who pleasured themselves
Pushing my body to theirs
Like a ragged doll
Like the one I used to play with
As a child
And then it was stolen
I'd let them
Because i was a open fridge
For anyone to reach in and grab
To quench their thirst
I think you were supposed to teach me
That love is not a selfish human habit
It's not the man, who shakes you until
there's nothing to spend or
Even left to maybe give in the name of generosity
It's the one who says
That there's nothing wrong
With just talking

- i think you did a really bad job

Pretty boys

I've had this love on my mind
Since my first heartbreak

When you
Finally let him go
Do it at once
Cold turkey
Your heart
Has proclaimed
Him liver

- he grows back

I've been running around
To feel good
So, I've had a lot of sex
With them
For a little
Love

- but, the love leaves too when they leave

The boys always ask me
Why they cant touch my face
I wouldn't tell them
That I'm hiding a garden
Full of prickly cactuses
On my chin

- secrets

I'm on a impatient hunt
Of finding a man
Before time runs out
Survival mode
I'll give you flowers
To profess affection
It is the only one way
That I know how to love
It is the best way
I know to escape
Myself

- to all the men I've given flowers

How does it feel to be inside of me
Do you feel my insecurities push you away
Every time you thrust forward

- turn off the lights

All you want is a way to
The part of my body
Where my legs meet my torso
You want to shove your hands
Where my legs meet my torso
And make yourself
Excited
With your eyes
Curled backwards
And your fingers finding a rhythm
You want to drink
The drama
Pouring out of my gaping hole
With your sharp pointy teeth
Why don't you
Hold me first
Why do you hurry

Mother
Don't shelter me so much
That they treat me like a puppet
When they meet me
Don't shelter me so much
That when they lie to me
I can't see their noses grow
Pinocchio
Mother
Don't shelter me so much
That I think their
Heart sits like mine
It beats like mine
It talks like mine
Mother
It thinks like mine

He tells me
Let's make memories
And I'm angry
I drink to that
But he looks so beautiful
Lying on my green bed
With his hands
Planted behind his head
And that subtle hint
Of a cocky smile
In his eyes
He dressed his face to seduce me
And that makes me smile

The first time I fell in love
With him
There was no love
Just a deep desire for acceptance
And a blinding want for perfect love
And picture perfect photos
That i could hang up in my house
In vintage floral frames
And stick into the plastic pockets
Of picture albums
Like the ones you could find in
Souvenir shops in Seattle
And my mother's closet at home
So, that when people came over
For milk tea
They would witness the love i was
Fortunate to have
They would beg to take some
Of the photos with them
And a few decades down
You'd find the photos
In thrift stores
Enough to be fought over
And bought with money
Because what I had was art

- because I wanted to be known as someone's loved one

This new tall boy
With the side swept hair
And the honey tongue
Kind of looks
like my interesting
English teacher
From high school
Tall boy
What does your heart think

- i talk with butterflies biting my stomach

It's calm now
During my favorite time
Of the day
When the sun
Hesitates to leave
It never leaves easily
Scars of pink, orange
And red
Are smeared across
Earth's canvas
I wish you were my sun
And I was yours
Then, we'd live with
Pink, orange and red
Emotions
You'd be my favorite
Time of the day

He had a summer heart
He could warm your days

- to perfect weather

I lean in
To kiss
Him on the forehead
He smells of
Kindness
God, He understands
My heart
He waits throughout
The self sabotage
He smells
Like an
Electric heart

- background junoon electric guitar sound

Let me be as close to you
As are your two fingers to each other

- then I`ll have conversations with you

Age 23

He loves my fingers
Slipping into his mouth
He says it's
What makes him
Feel electric
Then,
When he speaks
He is velvet
Velvet
When you run your fingers
Across him
Your hands leave prints
He doesnt agitate

- he's my first man

I unzip my yellow dress
For you
Let it fall to the floor
I look at you
Looking at me
And this time
I don't flinch

She isn't the prettiest person
That you'll ever know
But, the way that she looks at you
Will make you feel like
The prettiest person in the room

- she has tunnel vision

I can't stop boasting about you

Your face is as beautiful
As watching movies
On cold rainy nights
In empty theaters
High

- you make me think of unusual forest magic

Bad at taking pictures
But, I could be
Your muse

- you make me want to be wilderness

Those who have wandering on their mind
Are minimalists
They don't like keeping too many
Emotions around
They look for homes
In people
With foreign drinking habits
Chase thrill
Like kleptomaniacs
Who are crazy about the
Heart shaped pillow
You have in your room
You'll find them
In new places
With strange sounding languages
They
Will always take you
To the best places
And then leave you
To wander some more

Places that make you
Feel like
You lived your entire life
Just to be here

- when he takes you along

A love like
The love playing
On the cassettes
That we would listen to
On our road trips
To canada

- childhood trips

He says I should be
A bit more comfortable
In my own skin
He looks at my eyes
And secretly smiles
To himself
And then twirls me around
At staples street
Where it doesn't stop
Raining
He smells of pretty bonfires
And no goodbyes

I trace his masculine face
With my fingers
Memorizing every dip and shape
For my bad days

I want you
I breathe you
Through the window
Of my heart
That I keep open
With a single block of wood
For you
Because I like you
And then
I like you
A little more than like

That night
We kissed
Until blood
Dripped down
Our mouths

- virgin

I fell in love with the front zipper of his pants
And the sound of it opening

There is friction
In our words
When we talk
Our insecurities
Rub against each other
Like my brown thighs
When I walk
Why do we waste precious time
When there are plenty
Of better things to rub

I am not here to make a list
Of all the ways that
You are flawed
I am here to hug
All of you

- make up after a fight

You do have
A room
In my heart
But, you are
A guest
And I
Am
The owner

- landlord-tenant laws apply

You wait for
Me to love you
Then, you stop
Thinking about love

- ego and demons

He leans to the left
When he walks
It's a heavy heart
It's a heavy heart

- a boy in a man's body

The boys who don't know
How to give good hugs
Are usually the ones
Who need them the most

You make promises
To stay
With your eyes
Until you know she
Believes you
She hands herself
To you
Inside, out
In the name of love
Because women
Love the hardest
Then, you leave
Claiming
No strings attached
And she sits there
Becoming a sofa bed
Folding into herself

- she hasn't stopped folding for years

I've been running around trying to find you
In strange men
Who say all the things I want to hear
I blush cherries because of them
In strange men
Who chase me
With their hearts broken
By the last girl
I'd be their foundation
For a renewed home
In strange men
Who find better
When they feel better

- i'm bitter

I hope she breaks your heart
And you fall down from your
High building
Onto my bed,
And kiss me like how
You've pictured kissing her
In your head
And look at me
Like I'm all that
You've ever wanted
And smile
Like i give a second life to the
First butterflies in your stomach
I would stitch your heart back
With my superior love

- promises

I know exactly who she is
And yet, I bloat up with
Envy
And I can't stop looking at her
When she walks by
Is it her dresses
The way she parts her hair
The red lipstick that she smears
Onto her open lips
Mine are always fuller
Or is it the way she doesn't pay
Attention to you
That makes you hungry
And me the other woman

Then, I wonder
How could everything
That I've ever wanted
Not be wanted

Sometimes you change
For them
Without even noticing
You start to say all the things
That they might like to hear
And shy away from your own words
Because they're your dream man
And you're afraid that you'll never
Find one again
But, if you have to do that
Sweetheart
Lose yourself for someone
Know that they are no prince
They're just a jumping green frog

Don't chase him
Decorate yourself
With brown paint on your eyelids
And kohl in your eyes
And lavender butter on your skin
And bangles on your wrists
And witty words on your tongue
And playfulness in your bright eyes
And wind in your hair
And laughter
And laughter
And look away
When he looks at you
Because he is not
The one

At the end of the year
I come across all the tickets
That I purchased
To come see you
I crumple them up

As my heart breaks
I want this world to break too
I want the sky
To start showing cracks already
I want all the people to stop
Doing what their doing
And watch the sky mirroring
My heart
I want faces lifted in awe and despair
And fear
Of how you made me feel
And then, I want them to hate you

- the way you made me hate myself

I don't need you to feel beautiful
I don't, shouldn't, need you to kiss my body
Every inch of it
All the blemishes
All the dots
The deflated balloon skin
All the stretch marks
That rise higher and higher
Like kites in windy spring
Kiss my put together parts
To feel as if the world embraces me
And gives me the okay
To walk with anger, entitlement
And wit
I should need my strengthening words
And my bullet eyes
I should need my wholeness
I should need a conversation with me

- but I find myself having conversations with you in my head

When he tells you
That he doesn't want you
I don't want you to pity
Yourself
Don't count on him
To increase you in value
Know you are valuable
Regardless
You are whole
Regardless
Weren't you before him

- Is this love or ego

Life is easier
When you let go
When you are supposed to

When you love and like yourself
You don't need anyone else
To love and like you

I've lost you
In dimly lit bars
Staring at lights
That look like the sun
Shining in the night

I've forgotten you
In long train rides home
In long walks home
After a hundred conversations
And countless reassuring smiles
After finding people, who have shown me
That there are better hearts
That there are bigger hearts

Sometimes the boy deserves your affection
Sometimes you're just obsessive

Whenever you look at me
I know your heart quakes
With the what ifs
That you repeat to yourself
On your walks home
After work
You always take the long way home
And wait for the walk sign
Even when there aren't cars on the road
You hear about love
From your friends
Constant reminders of how
We don't talk
Then, you reach home
You hang up the tired what ifs
Alongside your coat
To wear them for the next day

- and the months keep passing by, darling

God won't
Lay him in your lap
If he isn't the one

- no matter how many dandelions you blow

Don't try to prove yourself to people
Your heart was not made
To be shredded and given out
For sampling

But, my sweet self
How do you expect other people
To know the inside of your mind
When you constantly change it
To what they might want to see

- losing authenticity

I want you to look at me
Like maybe
I am the traveler
Sought after
Sun
Running around
On the ground instead
Then
I'll set
in your bed
I'll set

- and you'll melt

Pretty boy
You'd have to climb
The hills of my heart aches
To meet me
Are you ready

- future lovers

I cover these holes
In me
Frantically
With my palms
So, you don't
See all
The spaces
I'm wanting
You to fill

- relationships

I will love you differently
Now
Not the sort of love
Where you eat me
Whole
And I am starving

- self love

To men
Who do not treat women
As vessels to be filled
Because we overflow
Milk tea in saucers
Warm and hearty
As candy that would be
Cleaner if it was wrapped
That don't describe women
As bees
Who are easy if they buzz
Or have locker room talks
That would have their mothers
Womb
Shrink in shame

- thank you

So, my mother says that you never forget
The boy who holds your hand first
But, i'll tell you
My mother held my hand first
When I needed that christmas hat
When I was in the chorus
Singing with my friends
In fifth grade
She lost her favorite
Ring that rain stained night
But, I never saw anger on her face
She held my hand first
When it was my birthday
And she knew I loved dolls
So, instead of going home from school
We went to the doll store
She held my hand first
When that boy said I couldn't
Catch him
And I got hit by the car
Because I've always
Been rust stubborn
She held a towel
To my face
When her face
Seemed more drained
And she held my hand first
Whenever we crossed the street
Green light, red light,
We held our hands tight
We were almost one
Brown together
My lover from birth

- first love

I don't regret you
To think of
Someone
Like every cell in your body
Is vibrating in uniform harmony
For their existence
Like vibrating stars
In the sky
Becoming selfless
To the extent of selfishness
Is freedom
Being thoughtful
Maybe like God
Is worship
Prayers for people are free
Love won't cost you a penny
You won't ever get
Poor
By giving either

Pretty boy
I have chased you
My entire life
To escape my body
So that you could
Make me feel
Good
Because my body
Never did
And now I sit here
Learning
And feeling
That my body doesn't need
To look good
For it to feel good
It is good

- regardless

Sitting during
One of those warm nights
Where I cry
Remembering
All of my heartbreaks
Starting from you

He asks me
How do I still
Have hope
In love
I tell him
I think with my heart
Babe

And you don't even know
Sometimes, wishes aren't granted
Because you didn't pray hard enough
Sometimes, wishes aren't granted
Because you did

Pakistan

Visiting my uncle's house
My sister and I with our small frames
But, puffy bellies
We eat
My uncle says, we should eat less
Young girls aren't supposed to be too heavy
No man would marry us
My sister gets mad

- securing husbands at ten

Age 8

She's leaving
Her dad's taking her to Pakistan
For a better life
Away from skimpy clothes
And women who talk back
Like the white women
Who never get married
Or have children
You'll see them saying
Namaste at the end
Of every sentence
She's going
To grow up better
Where everyone speaks
Her mother tongue,
I look out of my window
Down below in the night
Her brown car's getting smaller
As its rolling away
On the road
And I say goodbye to the small car

- best friend

Treasure boxes

Shalwar Kameez are so unpredictable
I love how you could add laces to it
Cut it from here
Stitch it from there
Give it an out of the box design
You're basically an artist
A mastermind
The laces are always so pretty
I've started collecting the different colored beads
But, only from the clothes that have been worn out
Strictly
There are little pink ones that look like seashells
And little flower shaped cut outs
That reflect the rainbow in them
I love them, all
Maybe not equally though
Like grandmothers
And their sons
My favorite are the red ones
That look like little barrels
I have around four handful of these now
I've purchased a small brown treasure box
From the gift shop
The one right across from my house
I keep them safe in there
They look like magic beads
Lucky beads
Sometimes I think they are

We step out of our house
My sister, my mother and I
Everyone stares
So many eyes on us
I can't count them all on my fingers
Men keep staring
Why are they staring
I don't think we look too great
Men have their eyes stretched
Elastic waistbands
Looking our way
Never looking away
We have puffy bellies
They stare
Mother makes us cover our
Heads and breasts with large chaadars
They stare
The road is crowded with
Carriages and other vehicles
One man with a moustache
Is riding his motorcycle
But, he's looking at me
And I can't stop staring at him too
His head is turned towards me
He almost hits a car
He looks at me one last time
To say bye
Perhaps
I don't understand

Age: 15

Dance the pounds away
If I move my body enough
It gets thinner
Mother says I'm thinner
I do laps around our house with my sister
Twenty-five to be exact
My sister does fifty
She is stronger
Beads of sweat slide down my temple
As I sprint
It's pretty hot here
Pakistan is scorching warm during the summer days
The most intense of it's four seasons
The electricity goes out often
But, when there is light
We turn on the radio
We have a lot of different colored cassettes
Full of 90's bollywood music
It's music for the lovers
But my brother and I
We dance
We create dance
I always teach him one of my favorite
Dance steps
It's a specific one
He's impressed
I'm a good dancer
He's alright

- boredom and losing weight

Six azaans
From the different mosques
That circle my house
Wake up the little birds before me
Before mother
Makes her morning tea
With the kitchen window open
Letting in cool air that foreshadows
Sweaty foreheads on school grounds
Near my window
The birds sing with the azaan
In their own languages
But they use the same words
Mother stays up with the birds
Mother loves to wake up
Mother sings to me to wake up
Like the birds

- morning mother calls

Don't tell me to stay out of the sun
To try out this new whitening
Cream that you've
Purchased for me
Like your mother did for you
So, that I'd glow
Brighter than milk tea
But, it isn't my cup of tea
And I don't need men talking about me
If I have to change for it
My skin is the cloth I never take off
I am full of it

- my brown is pretty too

Women wearing the brightest
Colors of loose fabric
On their sun admired
Glistening skin
The sun colored their skin
The aftermath of love making
He's a possessive man
A jealous man
He wants everyone to know
What's his
Generations of loving
The same milk tea woman
But, they still think it's infatuation

- sun loving

The first time
My dad told my mother
To shut up
Because he was
The roof above her head
She escaped to
the children's room
And she leaned against
The hard wall
That separated her
From my dad
And the love of her life
And she covered
Her face
Like a child
To hold the tears
Or do people do that
Because they feel alone
But like an overflowing
Glass of water
Under an open faucet
Her hands gave in
And we saw a puddle of an identity
On the floor
Looking at us
Observing us
Almost angry at us
She slid down the wall
Barren
So, did her pride and arrogance
In being who she is
Unapologetically

- the world owes you a hundred apologies

My mother has a garden in Pakistan
You'll find her in the summer sun
With her kameez lifted from the back
Because when the sun makes love to her
She sweats unconditionally
You'll see her digging the ground
To make room for
A new coriander plant
And eyeing for weed
And unwanted insects
Like a worried single mother
Who overthinks about strange men
Standing near the gate of her house
My dad doesn't live with us
He's in another country
To pay the bills
So, my mother falls in love with
Singers instead
At least for the time being
And writes young love letters
About their tunes
Because that's what people do
When their hearts break
By voices coming from
The other end of cell phones
They listen to music
That understands
Reassures
And listens back

Women who stay
For their children
I know that it would've been
Better if you left
But, thank you
For being a lover
Thank you for
Being a war heroine

- one woman army

What is love that
Cuts off your wings
Grooms you well
And places you into a
Cage to look pretty
When you were made
To have deep dimples
In your cheeks
And creases near your eyes
In the open wind
Sifting through the wind
Like an airplane
Sideways then
Balanced again
Rejoicing in the thrill
Lighting up the path
Wherever you travel
What is love that
Does not have perspective
Isn't thoughtful
Isn't considerate
Isn't free

Five years have ended

We're going to go back to the states
Soon,
So, I've started
Memorizing the dictionary
And I repeat the english phrases
That I hear the
Cartoon characters say
On t.v.
Because, I stutter sometimes
When I talk
I want to be prepared
I've read these words before
In novels
But, sometimes
I pronounce them wrong

- i'm scheduled for a culture shock soon

It is true that one of the worst things that could happen to you in Pakistan, is you having a little extra fat in you. It's almost as bad as not being a virgin, getting raped, or getting acid thrown on your face by spiteful cousins. Relationships don't work. It's hard getting married. They don't make bigger clothes for you, they make you hate yourself, until you don't have any self esteem to talk with. That's how they silence you. Until, you say yes to any man, even a married man with a child. The society is made to define women through a narrowed sense of beauty, as most societies are. Women are taught from an early age, that you need to look a certain way for approval. In contrast, this pressure isn't placed on a man at all. The way he looks, isn't judged or analyzed to decide if he makes the cut. Women are taught to look at themselves through the eyes of men, as if women should be desired and needed by men, as if women are supposed to be needed, as if you need to be needed.

To the country
That has taught me
Self-discipline
In polishing my shoes
Every morning
Before the sun wakes up

The country
That holds
Genuine friends
Who talk about the
Right things

The country
That has melody
That makes you
Let go
Of all the lovers
That lie
Because
The world is abundance

The country that gave me
A home
And continues to
Every time
I feel that I'm losing
Myself

- pakistan

You remind me of people in Pakistan

You'd hear a warm
Slow breeze that travels at night
Through cracked windows
To children holding candles
To ruffle their hair
For being good to their mothers
And to women standing on
Rooftops after a full day of
Taking care of their kids
On rooftops that are open to
The unpredictable sky and it's jewels
Like hearts that are capable of being open
Even after

Thoughts, questions and coping

I don't want to
Go home
With my mind
I don't want to
Think anymore

- let me go home with yours

Go away
To get rid of thoughts
You replace them with better thoughts

- recordings over recorded tapes

I'm too aware to stay depressed
So, I don't have the
Excuse of young naivety
Anymore
But, I'm too young to have clarity

- dilemmas

You have to believe in
That person that you want to
Become
Like you believe in God
And you believe in love
You can't see Him
But you know He's there

- faith

I twirl in my room
Like my friend twirls
Near the waters
In manhattan
Because he thinks a lot
Then he colors in books
That have cartoons in them
Similar to the ones I would
Watch as a child
In the 90s

- he likes the color red

I'm really hard on myself
So, as soon as I wake up in the morning
I say two things
I thank God for all that He has given me
And I ask myself for forgiveness
I don't know why it's helping me
But it is
And I feel okay

I'm wilting
It's not something
You could see
Because I color my
Discolored petals
Yellow every morning
So, I look like the sun to
You
I fake it through the day
So, you feel better

- ritual

I don't want to be heard
Or seen sometimes
And I
Dont
Think
That's normal

I don't want to feel like you snatched
My power
Of making decisions
I'll pretend that I gave it to you willingly
It is the closest that I've gotten to
Schizophrenia

- coping mechanisms

Yes, I have been soiled
Hello, I'm not the untouched woman
That you want and desire
I am the slut
That opens her legs
When you press her button
I moan
And scream
Until the moon is a shy man
He can't look me in the eye
For too long
I wink and I whistle
Until they tell me I need to act like a woman
I look at you with laughter in my eyes
Before you look at me
With laughter in your eyes
Because you are no lion
Because I am no sheep

- coping mechanisms

Now a days
I've started walking
Like a man
So, you wouldn't think my
No is a yes
Or even a maybe

- intimidation game

Depression is a calm lover
Maybe, that's why I always go back
To him
Or maybe it's something that he does
With his hands
He has mischievous eyes
But, he holds me like he loves me
Like, I'm his whole world
Codependency
Unhealthy relationships
But, he gives me the attention
I crave
Stockholm syndrome
You'll always catch me rubbing
My cherry against him
And kissing him
To misery

I'm going to be
In the newspaper tomorrow
The way these people note me
I've been pushed on a stage
But, I've never really been into theatre
I'm one and they're twenty minds
They'll make a circle around me
And laugh at me
For all the ways
I'm not similar to them
I'll be an outcast soon
Or am I already
Face readers?
I smile to look calm
I sit on this bench
Aware of every movement
I make
I'm
Trying to focus
On my reading
My ears are drumming
Beat, beat, beat
And I don't know where
To look
My eyes are wide open
Alert
Ready for them

- social anxiety

I hold my tightened fist to my heart and
I say
I am strength
I've done it before
I'll do it again
I'll be better soon
I'll know better soon

- do it with me

I've been walking on
This tightrope
Balancing on this tightrope
Change compartments in trains
Focused
Learning from it
Trying not to lean on one side
Too much
But, I do sometimes
In the fear of
Doing it incorrectly
Self sabotage
But, I am certain now
I listen to my mind
I listen to my intuition
When you listen to your intuition,
It gets comfortable with you
That's when it opens up to you
It tells you secrets
Secrets you were the first
To hear

- most of us just want to be listened to

Over thinking
Is cancer
There was a thought
That was only supposed to be
Read once
But you have sat down now
With your notebook
To interpret it
Like a student
Breaking down poetry
You treat these words
As if they are arabic verses
They have more than one meaning
But, what you read is a reflection
Of your insecurities
Of how people have treated
You
It's your fears
Speaking now
In your voice

- but, your voice was only supposed to belong to you

Mirrors are like people
They lie

- you see what you think, so know what you think

The voices in my
Head
They're so loud
That I can't study
There's a herd of people
Protesting
A battle ground that
Has been set up
On one side
They root for me
And on the other
They want me to
Be captured
But, I'm a war hero
I repeat to myself
A war heroin

You tell me to
Open this book
And read
But
The ceiling is open
And the rain is pouring
My dress is wet
And I can't focus

Where do I find God
So, I could tell Him to do
One of those things
That He does best
Snap his magician fingers
And make my dreams come true
It is so easy
To snap fingers
Just one swift fast motion
And be I'll be saved
Of unusual pacing habits in small rooms
And involuntary legs that move on their
Own accord when I think too much
I don't want to reach
For my head anymore
God
To sit in despair
That crawls on the bridge of my spine
It's an itsy-bitsy spider
My God
It never knocks

- where is the satellite that connects us to God

The eve of every six months
I cry
I still haven't been able to know why
I think its bottled emotions
Like piled up clothes
In the corner of my room
And dirty dishes stacked
Up in my sink
I never knew that I bottled emotions
I can't stop
And I don't know how to stop
So, I give in, until
I wring out the heated
Dirty water in me

- doing laundry

By the eight cigarette
I'm lying on the park bench
Looking up at the sun quitting
For the day
Mother is waiting at home
But, I'll go once
I see the sun out

- my manners

When the sun starts to set
I quickly run to the bathroom
Gargle, wash my face
Then I wash my feet in the sink
Like I used to as a child
In the masjid that I would go learn
Quran
I find my hooded cape hanging on the
Hook behind my door
I hurriedly put it on
Making sure no hair shows
I lay the prayer mat
In the direction that everyone does
I close the light
Then I write letters to God
With my fountain pen
So, the smudged ink
Blares hard work
Impressionable
And when It's time to ask for
What I want
I whisper
God, make me prettier
And I know it's the wrong thing to ask
Because I've asked for greater things
But, even in this sun lit
Orange room
Where life seems divine
And the angels are about to have a meeting
Fit for kings
And it seems like my magic beads are finally working

- that's how he makes me feel

Don't base your worth on
Someone's capability of
Remembering you
It is not directly proportional

- my grandma's memory

You need space of mind
To consider the self love
You lack in your life

- make space

I don't feel good
I don't feel pretty
I don't feel important
I feel embarrassed
And humiliated
I feel inadequate
And not in control
I don't fit in now
I feel like you know what
Makes me feel small
I've hid it for so long
But, now, you see it
I know you do
And that makes me want
To fold

There was a first
Pretty? You're not
Now, it echoes
Back and forth

Let's correct
All the ways
That you stitched and sewed
Yourself wrong
I know you were
In a hurry
But, now we have made the time

All anger is
Not harmful
Frustration isn't
Unease
Anger is healthy
It allows you to
Fight
And
Open and pounce
Like cornered tigers

- freedom

We should be like
The sun and its venting and being
Angry
And being stubborn

- beauty happens when you let it out

I think you should make your life a little
More colorful
Grab a paintbrush
Draw the sun on the corner, yellow
Then, a river in the center, blue
And finally, mountains
In the back, grey
Then light it up
And make a wish
And let it fly to the pink sky

- imagining

Keep re-doing your life
Until you get it right

- you'll get it right

Comfort in discomfort
But, first
You have to get used to it

In order to be found
You must be lost
The deeper that you are lost
The greater that you see
The greater that you have
When you are finally found

- let go of control, but know you have it

Your life is a stencil
Use discipline
To fill it
And let the extra endings
Fall away

My room is messy
It's still air
Here
Silent homemakers
It's still
Like tall buildings
That stand quiet
Like children who
Try not to cry
When they see
Their siblings
Getting hit by their
Father
Question
Does cleaning your room
Give you clarity
Or does clarity help you
Clean your room
Does your impulsive decision of
Seeing neatness
Lead to your thoughts lining up in order too
There's unwashed laundry
On the corner
It's been there for a month
The days pass by fast
Maybe, we should start
With that pile

- beginnings

I'm not fond of questions
But, I do want my answers

When a caterpillar
Becomes a mature butterfly
My darling
It changes its habits
What it eats
What it chooses to surround itself with
You are no different

- growth

God didn't create
You with one
Purpose
For the sole reason
Of having your virginity
How could such a great
Creation
Have only one way of being valuable
There are greater
Purposes
Men say that you
Lost it
Something sour
Something that makes
You want to go find it again
That's how men phrase it
My woman
This hole of yours
Is not a possession
It's a place
You define it
It'll never be lost

- private property

Age 23

I asked her
How are you so calm and zen like
And she told me
It's because
Of all the people that
She met
They had given her zen
And I just kept thinking
That night
And I couldn't stop thinking
Until morning hit my curtains
I wish I met all the people
She met

Saying no to all the things
You have to
You'll get all the things
You need

Be careful of how you choose to draw
Yourself
When you're asked to
Because that's how they'll draw you
When they're asked to

I hope you find that miracle
That makes you want to
Keep going

Doubt in your writing is something
That shows itself
Only when you forget to hold on
To your thoughts

- doubt is a foreign thought

I think it is the time
Around your early twenties
That you should be ready to create
Your most honest art
You have the adults living and a
Child's heart

I need inspiration

- then retrace your steps

I write
I sit down and rub hydrogen peroxide
On my wound
I write
I sit down and rub hydrogen peroxide on my wound

Let your regrets
Slip in through
The little cracks
In you
Absorb them
Like pavements
That are sat
Open for rain water

- that's how flowers grow

So, you saw failure
Now, the easiest way to avoid failure
Is to convince yourself that
You don't want that thing anymore
Because you like something else now
But your heart still mentions it to you
On train rides home
During sincere conversations
In ambitious eyes
Although, it whispers it
Because it's afraid that
You'd get mad
Because you show mediocracy
And expect an A for effort
You cover your heart again
To silence it
That ritual that you do every night
And turn to the other side of the bed
And close the lamp

- demoralized

Hey you
Don't be the person who doesn't run for the bus
Because you're afraid to feel embarrassed
That you might miss it
Hey, you, if you don't run you'll never know
If you could've sat in it

- giving up without trying

On the other side of all the things
That make you feel fear
And sit you in the lost and found
There is a happily ever after

- walk to the other side

Sometimes you'll twirl
Because you want to
Sometimes bad times
Will make you twirl
And twirl

- but you'll feel lighter

Who made you believe
That you're supposed to hide
Parts of you
That you think aren't lovable

- embrace

When they tell you to
Love yourself
They never tell you how
So, I'll tell you how
First, take yourself out
Tonight
To your most favorite place
Mine is the Brooklyn bridge
If you want to dress up, do that
But it's fine, if you don't
And, before you get there
Get yourself some waffles
From the truck nearby
To sweeten your time
And as you walk, feel your body
The one you've lived with
Since you had memory
Acknowledge that it's yours
And its attached to you.
And look up at the lights
The ones that never turn off at night
And feel time hurrying by you
As you hurry by the
Few people who would be the last
To reach home
Then, find your favorite bench
And stay there for as long as you wish
It's that simple
And there's no hurry
There never is
And you don't need to think anymore
The lights are lit up
They're thinking for you
And it's all alright

175

Being okay in your skin
Is a freedom
That was always yours
To accept

- acknowledging

When you try to fit in
You try to escape yourself
Escape all the parts that you think
Aren't lovable
Instead, why don't you
Know yourself
Then memorize yourself
Like arabic verses
From the Quran
And recite yourself
Until their ears perk up
Because of all the noise
And excitement
Until they pick up
Your catchy tune
Then teach them
About yourself
Because you
Know yourself
And have
Memorized yourself
Teach them how to fit in
With you

You have to be open to accomplishing the smaller goals that you have. No, don't shove them to the side because you have bigger dreams to focus on at the moment. You're tired of doing small things, and you're frustrated. Yeah, frustrated is a better word. But, the small goals are setting stones to the bigger ones. Five smaller goals accomplished makes one big goal accomplished. Humble yourself, discipline yourself and learn about the art of waiting. And if you could be patient while you wait, that would be great too.

Don't hate your current moment
It is the only bridge to the next

Age 19

People would tell me
That there are no sudden shifts
It's not like how it happens in the movies
It's different
But, that's how it happened to me
Or maybe, I just get bored easily
I think I got bored of being tired
Or just doing the same thing
Over and over again
And so, I decided that I wanted to live
Differently
And experience something new
And feel something new
I wasn't really trying to save myself
I was just trying to learn
How to live differently

Tired
Of doing the same things
Over and over again,
Then everything slowed down again,
A lot of things weren't happening at once anymore
So, I could keep up
It gave me space to think
It was one of those summer nights
With the warm wind and pink sky
At ceasars bay
The place my parents would bring
Me often, to get excited about toys
In the toys r us nearby
And when the wild wind ran towards me
I ran towards the wind
I ran until I was the wind
And i was excited again
And I was a child again

- and I was in control again

Age 24

Tonight
I'll take a bath
I'll wash my hair
I'll shave my legs
Ill scrub my back
With my loofah
Then, I'll walk down the stairs to my room
I'll turn on some classic Nazia Hassan music
And then I'll find green string to thread my mustache
Then, I'll take lavender butter
And massage my whole body
I'll make sure I don't miss a spot
Because, I want pretty skin
And then before I lay on my back
I'll take a spoon full of acceptance
But, I'll make sure it's the pink medicine
That I loved when I was a child
Because the bitter one is not soft
To my tongue
I'll close my eyes
And think of Mother
And I'll drift off to sleep

- the simplest nights

I blow a kiss to you
During my favorite
Time of the day
For all that you've endured
Giving up at times,
Prevailing the other times
I know you've witnessed both
You're like me
Not perfect
Living the human experience
Trying
And then trying
Some more

There is no quick fix for you
But there are fixes every day

Heart

When she laughs
Her face scrunches up
Until she is laughter
And laughter surrenders
It's will to her

- flower face

Here's to all the heartaches
That keep your heart gentle
Jelly
And clean
And arrogantly honest

- cheers

For all the what ifs that you
Keep hidden in your heart
And all the maybes that accidentally
Slip out of your tongue
Skip the vigil tonight
Because there is no such thing
As the one who got away
People who are supposed to
Belong in your life
Things that are supposed to be
Present
Are
Because life, at every moment
Has been exactly
How it was supposed to be

Turn your face away
From anything that disrupts
The peace in your heart
As the law of vacuum states
Let go
So
You could
Let in

- or better yet, let gone

How do I fix a
Broken heart
I asked her
And she said
With a voice as soft
As my mother's hand
In my hair, coaxing
Me to sleep

Open your heart
Even further
Like the bookstores
You'll find in small towns
That have blue bordered
Open signs
Stuck to their
Windows
Regardless of the rain,
Regardless of the night,
Reassuring you, that you'll
Find a safe place within
Let people
Stay, and read
For a while
Don't usher them out
Too soon
And when you feel fear at the
Hollow of your throat
I want you to swallow it
And tell it,
That everything is fine
And that you may hate a
Thing and it is good for you
And you may love a thing
And it is bad for you

If you compare
The yellow dress that
You wear
To someone else's dress
If you compare the
Colorful beads
From your treasure box
Sewn into your dress
To the crystals taylored into
Someone else's
You strip yourself from
Your dress
You give it away
By choice
And I know how much
You love yours
You'd never want to give it away
So, don't sit pouting near the window
Sulking
When you know
How the world works
And how it doesn't

- tough love is dad's love

Then I take the flower
That the rain made damp
I shred it with my hand
I ruffle it into my hair
I love my hair and pink flowers
Then I take the green leaf
I crush it into my hand
Then my nose
Smells my hand

- it smells like all the secrets of the world

To heal
I find people
In paper
In ink
In minds
And I look at their
Oddly shaped Hearts
That look oddly like mine

- read

It is easy to talk in foreign countries
People don't hide emotions
To look normal
They don't call you cute or pretty
They tell you that you're beautiful
They write their words on their skin
And hang them on their balconies
For everyone to see
And I think that's what true freedom is

- there isn't a stage and no one puts on a show

We've all had pretty moments
You can't wave them off
Just because they were with people
You didn't end up with
Experience is time well spent
Time is never wasted
But, pain is
So, learn from it
Take your receipts wherever you go
And color them too
And make them look pretty
Because they are

You're holding a microphone
And are about to sing
The verse that makes people
Scream at the top of their lungs
But only you know why you wrote the verse
And what you really meant

- poetry

I'm a dervish
For my art
So, you could
Feel disreputable
Faith in me

Believe in God
And
Believe God

The prayer that is heard the clearest
Is thank you

When we finally meet
I promise, I'll recognize
You by how
Clean you choose to keep
Your heart
And we'll laugh so much
That we'll cry
And I know that even though
Life has never been
Perfect for me
You'll always be

You could go on
With your life
Even after
Maybe, you'll get better
Faster than I did
And find a new way
Of thinking
Maybe, you needed
To learn that you can't control
How life unfolds on you
Yet, you do have
Control on what you do
That's the biggest lesson

So, I'll sit here in my room
With my brother
And I'll pray for you
And your heart
And that when you find
Your heart breaking again
You understand it
And you love it even more
That you not be afraid of it
And not go numb to it
But, feel with it's broken skin
Healing, trying
For you
Follow it
Wherever it goes
Even if it's unfamiliar places

Age 6

When it rains on my block
You can't see anything clearly
It's a white drapery hanging
My sister and I are walking out of the building
That we've been living in for years
I love when it rains
I have boyish hair
We're about to play the shoe game
With pink and blue slippers
Were gonna put our shoes on the edge of the road
In the flowing stream
Its running really fast
My slipper is sailing away like a ship
We're running with the slippers
Like shooting airplanes in the sky
We've almost reached the end of the street
Were almost out of breath now
We get to the corner of the road
The slippers are standing at the gutter now
Tired like us
She picks hers up
I quickly pick mine
We run back to do it again

How do I make you feel
She asks me
And I look up
At the warm bluish sky
I point at the sun
With my two hands

- self love

I'm ready to go back now
Twirling in my yellow dress
Clutching my yellow flowers
To my chest
To give one to
Every single person
Who has hurt me
And I'll keep the ones
That are left
For myself

- forgiving

In writing this book, I fell more in love with all the people around me, my family, my friends and every other gem, I've come across. Sometimes, we forget all that the people in our lives do for us. I'm immensely grateful for these pretty souls in my life, and cannot find a thank you, that would do them justice. They have carved the person that I am, and have given me strength in unease. And you, I can't find a thank you, big enough for you either. But, still, thank you for reading me, thank you for being the friend that I've always needed. Thank you for listening to me, my new, kind friend and thank you my most favorite friend ever, for never telling me to stop.

I love you from the wholeness of my unwavering heart.